DANIEL

A Play

(Inspired by the biblical story of Daniel)

PHILIP BEGHO

Monarch Books

DANIEL

First Published 2001

copyright © **Philip Begho** 2001
All rights reserved

All rights in this play are strictly reserved. No performance or reading of the play may be given and no copy of the play or any part thereof may be reproduced, stored in a retrieval system, or transmitted in any form or by means, electronic, mechanical, photocopying, recording, or otherwise, without the prior written permission of the author, with the exception of brief excerpts in magazines, articles, reviews, etc.

All applications regarding the rights to this play (whether performing or otherwise) should be made to the author through his publishers.

Email: monarch_books@yahoo.com
Tel: +234 8060069597

ISBN 978-32224-1-4

PUBLISHED BY MONARCH BOOKS
NIGERIA

DANIEL

CHARACTERS

DARIUS THE MEDE, King of Babylon.

QUEEN HAJITHA, His wife.

DANIEL)
) The three chief administrators
SATALA)   of the
)   Babylonian Empire.
NIMRI)

ZABAK, The king's aide.

SCENE: The entire action takes place in a private chamber annexed to the king's court. About 537 BC.

Daniel was first presented by Monarch Productions at the MUSON Center, Lagos, on December 4, 1994, with the following cast:

KING DARIUS	Ayo Lijadu
QUEEN HAJITHA	Joke Silva
SATALA	Ihria Enakimio
NIMRI	Francis Onwochei
DANIEL	Femi Ogunjobi
ZABAK	Muyiwa Odukale

And

Toyin Oshinaike
Lillian Agbeyegbe
Adeniran Makinde

Directed by Jide Ogungbade
Costumes by Ogbemi Heymann
Lighting and set by Phillip Igetei
Make-up by Faith Egboigbe
Associate Producer: Lillian Agbeyegbe
Producer: Ayo Lijadu

Act 1

A private chamber annexed to the court of KING DARIUS. *It is lavishly furnished as befitting a reception chamber of the ruler of a great empire.*

No one present, except SATALA *and* NIMRI. NIMRI *paces the length of the chamber in high anxiety.* SATALA *watches him, amused. At length* SATALA *lets out a long mocking chuckle.* NIMRI *halts in his tracks and sends a suspicious look at him.* SATALA *stops chuckling and straightens his face.* NIMRI *begins to pace again.* SATALA *laughs,* NIMRI *looks at him.* SATALA *begins to pace in mocking imitation of* NIMRI, *and breaks into laughter.*

NIMRI: You laugh.

SATALA: Yes, Nimri, I laugh. I laugh.

NIMRI: Why?

SATALA:

What is there to do but to be at ease,

To laugh, be merry, kiss life upon the nose,

To whistle, raise the knee and do a jolly jig?
[*Demonstrates.*]

NIMRI:

But should the king refuse, Satala?

SATALA [*finding a bowl of wine*]:

And if perchance you find wine, to guzzle it;
[*Guzzles.*]
And if you find a woman – ha! – a woman...

NIMRI: Satala! Should the king refuse?

SATALA: He will not refuse, Nimri.

NIMRI:

He's a man, Satala, with astute faculties

And eyes accustomed to seeing through mists.

SATALA:

And a king; and like kings, he's flawed by pride.

NIMRI:

This scheme runs against the grain of my ways.

SATALA:

It's chiseled by most cunning artifice,
Sculpted for sure success. Nimri, it cannot fail.

NIMRI:

I'd sooner put a knife to Daniel's throat!

SATALA: Ssh! The king comes!
[*They listen and wait but no one appears.*]
It isn't him.
It's the uncouth, Nimri, the unrefined,
Who puts a knife to the throat of his prey;
Artifice rather gives him a bone to eat
That catches in his throat and pierces knife-deadly.

NIMRI:

But has the king truly marked him for this great rise?

SATALA:

My source is as good as the king's sober mouth.

NIMRI: It is madness!

SATALA:

For whom? Not for Daniel, surely; nor the king,
Nor for the realm, which would be festive glad
To see the last of us and our fell yoke:
Face it, Nimri, we milked the land not tenderly.

NIMRI:

Any would have done as we did, Satala.

SATALA: Daniel did not.

NIMRI [*groans*]: Daniel...

SATALA: Ssh!

Daniel

[*They shush up as they hear movements at the portals.*]

[*Enter* ZABAK *with wine.*]

Zabak, does the king come?

ZABAK:

He comes in a little while, my lords,

And sends his finest wine before him.

[*He pours out wine.*]

SATALA: Is this the king's finest wine?

ZABAK: His very best, my lord.

SATALA [*pointing to the bowl he emptied*]: As good as that?

ZABAK: Which, my lord?

SATALA: That.

ZABAK: Oh, the queen's cat's wine.

SATALA: W-what?

ZABAK: Yes, my lord;
The queen's new cat has a taste for wine.

SATALA [*spluttering, half-retching*]:
The queen's cat's wine?

ZABAK: The queen pampers him.
[*Offering him a goblet of wine*] My lord.

SATALA: No!

ZABAK: Lord Satala will not have wine?

NIMRI: The cat...

ZABAK: The cat?

NIMRI:
The cat has stolen his taste for wine.

Daniel

ZABAK [*now understanding*]: Ah...
[*He bows and leaves quickly so as not to burst into laughter in front of them.*]

SATALA: Oh, for the throat of that feline...

NIMRI:

I would rather our knives found Daniel's throat.
Satala, beware the ways of the self-righteous:
Those with neither courage nor shrewdness to grasp wealth
Hide their limp hearts behind the plea of uprightness,
And nurse a deadly envy for the stout-hearted,
Until the fortuitous visit of power
Gives thunder and striking arm to their hate,
And then it's 'Feed this man to the lions!'
If Daniel lives, Satala, you and I are dead.

SATALA:

Yes, if he lives, Nimri; if he lives.
But he will not live. I hold his death in my hand,
Bound, wrapped, and secured, in this little scroll.

NIMRI:

What do scrolls and Nimri have in common?
The glint and thrust of the assassin's blade
In hostile intrigues and war-like exploits
Have thus far wrought safe dispatch of my
    adversaries;
Let the glint of it, I say, Satala,
Now rid us of this adversary Daniel.

SATALA:

Though you affect the manner of a fool
I know you, Nimri, to be keen of wit,
Therefore lend us the use now of your wits:
If Daniel falls to the assassin's blade,
In whose camp would suspicion first alight
If not his rivals', those stumped by his lifting;
No, Nimri, this calls for cunning and artifice,
And cunning and artifice have spied the land
And all the ways and paths of Babylon,
And bear report that only in the matter
Of the law of his God may Daniel be ensnared.
No web or cunning snare will fetter his feet

Save one spun and sprung across the doors of his strength,
For in a man's strength does his weakness lie.

NIMRI:
Like the weakness that lies in your strong tongue?
Words, only words; what strength have you but empty words?
Satala, mark me well: this plan will fail!

SATALA:
Watch and see, Nimri, the power of words well wrought.

ZABAK [*offstage*]: The king! The king!
[*Enters.*]
Darius the Mede, King of Babylon!
[*Enter* KING DARIUS. *Exit* ZABAK.]

SATALA & NIMRI [*bowing*]:
Live for ever, O king!
Live for ever, Darius King of Babylon!

KING DARIUS: What brings you here,
Lords of Babylon, my chief administrators?

SATALA:
A most glad and happy matter, O king.

KING DARIUS:
A glad and happy matter? Glad and happy?
Has the impish god of gold then been found?
Do you bring him in captive bonds to my throne
To spew forth at my every toss of head
Enough yellow to wean the heart of my queen
Off affairs of state to trinkets and jewelery
And stuff as are women's proper concerns?

SATALA:
The king is wise and knowing as ever,
For we indeed bear gold, though not of wonted hue.
This, O king, is of inky black complexion,
But gold nonetheless of most precious value.
Here in my hand it lies, venerable king.

Daniel

KING DARIUS: A scroll...

SATALA:

A request from all the prefects and satraps
And officials, counselors and governors –
All you have appointed to administer
And rule over your vast and sprawling regions:
They request the king's decree forbidding all men
For the space of thirty days to bow in prayer
To any god or man, save you, O king.
Only to you, and to you alone, O king,
May men bow in petition or supplication.

KING DARIUS:

I have neither desired nor asked this honor.

SATALA:

The honor of men wears brightest on kings
When unasked, uncommanded, and unsought.

KING DARIUS:

You rank me with the gods of men, should this be?

SATALA:

The stretch of Babylon knows Darius fears no god.
All saw Darius the Mede gather Babylon
As a lion in prime gathers a buck,
And who could stop you? Nor man, nor Chaldean
   gods.

KING DARIUS:

The lion grows old, age creeps on me.

SATALA:

And with venerable age has honor grown:
Men who fear and honor gods, fear and honor more
He who fears no god, who in his conquering youth
Wore in his arm the ravage and thunder
Of the wrathful gods, but wears in his age
The gentleness and benevolence of the wise gods.
Such do men honor, and so for thirty days
Men will put aside their gods to honor as god
Darius the Mede, ruler of Babylon –
Babylon! The dread of the astonished world!

Daniel

KING DARIUS: Let me see the scroll.

SATALA: As the king pleases.
[*He hands it over and shows another scroll.*]
The decree. Prepared and awaiting the king's seal.

KING DARIUS:
The decree? Prepared already?
You presume, Satala! You presume!

SATALA:
I presume only, my lord, to honor the king,
And with dispatch and speedy grace, serve him.

KING DARIUS [*casting a glance at* NIMRI]: Nimri!

NIMRI: My king!

KING DARIUS:
You wear a strange and silent face.
What thoughts of malice wedge your tongue?

NIMRI: My king?

KING DARIUS [*eyes on the scroll*]: Speak, speak!

NIMRI:
Ah... ah... it's – it's a good plan, my king.

KING DARIUS: A good plan?

SATALA: He means, my king, he means –

KING DARIUS:
What does he mean? Nimri, speak!

NIMRI: My king...

KING DARIUS [*looking up from the scroll*]:
I see the names of the governors and satraps
And the names of my chief administrators –
The well-penned names of Satala and Nimri!
But I do recall, lords esteemed of Babylon,
That the amplitude of my empire

Daniel

Lays claim to three chief administrators.
Three, my friends, not two. Daniel, Satala...
Where is Daniel's name here? I cannot find it.

SATALA:
Daniel, as my lord the king may recall,
Is away touring on the king's business,
And though my lord the king may not know it,
In the ranks of the king's most loyal servants
Daniel stands in hew distinguished, princely cut.
'Tis but my debt to the king enables me
Thus efface myself and push his furtherance
Whose loyalty assumes such distinction
That once I saw him weep for want of means
To honor more the king's eminence.

KING DARIUS:
Letters from him hint a return today
In the wake of a mission well dispatched.

SATALA:
He returns today? What splendid news, O king!

Most welcome! The scroll will yet boast his name.

KING DARIUS:

Indeed, stay the matter and wait for Daniel,
If his name on the list will gladden him.
I've sent request for him to attend the king
At his earliest convenience upon his return.

SATALA: Agreed, my lord. Agreed.
[NIMRI'S *cup drops.*]

KING DARIUS:

Nimri, you've dropped your goblet.
What strange look wraps you?

SATALA:

I daresay 'tis the look of distrust.

KING DARIUS: Distrust? Zabak!

ZABAK [*offstage*]: O king!

Daniel

SATALA:
Nimri doesn't trust me, my king. See how he sweats!
[*Enter* ZABAK.]

KING DARIUS [to ZABAK]:
Let the physician attend; this man is sick!

NIMRI:
No, my king. No, Zabak. No. 'Tis but a trifle –
Nothing a little repair will not mend;
And I must repair home now, with the king's leave.
[*Bows and makes to leave.*]

SATALA:
No, wait! The king deserves an explanation.
Come now, Nimri, should we not make disclosure?

NIMRI: Satala!

SATALA:
Come, my friend, a little explanation
Is often good and prudent policy.

[ZABAK *attends to the spillage, bows and leaves.*]
As we came, my king, as we set course here –

NIMRI: Satala!

SATALA:
Be patient, my friend; a little patience
Is often the beam that lights the heart of mystery.

KING DARIUS:
Satala, my ears pine for your secrets. Speak!

SATALA:
Pardon, my king; pardon. As we set course here,
Nimri, being struck by thirst, fell to some wine.
[*He inspects the cat's bowl comically.*]
I cautioned thus: Nimri, patience! Patience!
Wait and have your fill of wine at the king's;
Drink not this, for at the king's you will drink,
And finest wine sits ill on lesser wine.
But Nimri trusted not my counsel
And the discomfiture born of his distrust

Now drives us all too soon from the king's presence.
[*Laughs.*]

KING DARIUS [*chuckling*]:
Wine! Ever the bane of princes!

NIMRI [*bowing, and grabbing hold of* SATALA]:
If it pleases the king, the hour begs us leave.

SATALA [*bowing*]:
Yes, we leave, with the king's indulgence.
[*They begin to leave, then* SATALA *wrests himself from* NIMRI'S *grip and backtracks to* KING DARIUS.]
My king, if I may take the scroll to Daniel
To enter his name himself, for that will please him.

KING DARIUS [*stretching the scroll to him*]:
Ah, yes...

SATALA [*not taking it*]:
A thought suddenly alights on me, O king.
It is much said by those of pensive minds

That the promise of a gift is sweet surprise
But a surprise bestowal is sweeter gift.
If this is so, if the proverb is true,
If the tongues of sages still birth wisdom,
Would not Daniel, spent by his journey's drag,
Stretched and fatigued by his labor's striving,
Zealous and certain in the king's concerns,
Of single mind with his master's desires,
Desirous of his master's honoring,
Not greet with greater joy a thing accomplished,
A decree signed, sealed and delivered?
My king, would not he? This Daniel that I know,
Would not he with more joy greet a deed
    accomplished
Honoring his master before the world and men,
Than all the promises of noble intentions –
Limping words on a crutch of lame proposals –
Saying, 'Thus do we intend, thus we do intend;
Thus and thus do we sincerely intend'?
My king, yes? Would not he? Would not Daniel?

Daniel

KING DARIUS:

Your tongue, Satala, rides a persuasive course
On words the very stallion of wisdom.

SATALA:

The stallion, to the common eye, is but a horse;
'Tis royal sight, made keen by more than
   diadem
That finds on the rude beast the stallion's silver
   mane.

KING DARIUS: H'm. I am won.

SATALA:

Wisdom smiled to have won so fair a prize, my king,
When she found you, cradle-tucked, and named you
   hers.

KING DARIUS:

I am won, Satala; I am won. The decree.

SATALA [*handing it to him*]: My king.

KING DARIUS [*signing and sealing it*]:
A thing done of a thing to be done
Is a thing less to be done, and much relief.
Here is your decree, my lords administrators,
Signed and sealed as you have entreated:
Who bows in supplication to any but me,
Who petitions any man or god but me
In the space of thirty days from this day
Has his life forfeit, and to the lions' den
Will be cast. I, Darius the Mede, have spoken.

SATALA [*taking the decree from him*]:
As you have spoken, O king,
As you have decreed and sealed, so shall it be done.
[*He turns to* NIMRI *and slaps him on the back with a chuckle.*]
To business, Nimri;
Or does your distrust still discomfit you?

SATALA & **NIMRI** [*at the door*]:
Live for ever, O king! Live for ever!
                    [*Exeunt.*

Daniel

KING DARIUS:

Satala, your words seem wise, but not so your ways.
When wise words scorn the path of wise ways,
There – is found a prodigy of mischief.
[*Pause.*]
As for Daniel ... Ah Daniel ... So ... so...
So, Daniel, faithful servant, so shall you
In the little space of one happy day
See the magnificence of two ample gifts:
One a gift of men to me and thus to you,
And one a gift from me, your king, to you –
Alone to you, yes my Daniel, alone:
The branch you bore with those two half-worthies,
Who beside your mighty cedar are mushrooms,
Alone now bear, and with the excellent spirit
I've found in you, have tried, tested and proved,
Govern my dominion, unyoked and unfettered.
[*Enter* HAJITHA *in time to catch the last lines of the above, with her cat in her arms.*]

HAJITHA:

Does my king talk and hold council with himself
As do the mad, or the old and lonely?

KING DARIUS: Am I not old and lonely?

HAJITHA:
You may be lonely, but you are not old.
No, my king, you're not old; for what is age
But a trick of vision, a false shadow
Cast by love's lack and dispelled by love's light.
My love for the king is as the unaging sun
Whose light sees ever the youth of love.

KING DARIUS: Hajitha, my lovely doe,
How tender and caressing are your words.

HAJITHA: No, my king, touch me not.

KING DARIUS: Hajitha...

HAJITHA: I am angry.

KING DARIUS: My queen?

HAJITHA: You are lonely.

KING DARIUS: Come now, my queen...

HAJITHA:
No. You're lonely. I'm here for you but you're lonely.

KING DARIUS:
Come, come ... Come, my lovely flower.

HAJITHA: I'm just a flower.

KING DARIUS: Hajitha ... Come...
Let me smell the delicacy of your fragrance.

HAJITHA:
Of what use is a fragrant flower to loneliness?

KING DARIUS [*chuckling, placating*]:
You know I said it in jest.

HAJITHA: I see ... Queen Hajitha
Has now become a jester's plaything.

KING DARIUS:

Will you not be appeased? Come, taste of this wine.

HAJITHA:

I'm drunk already to offense, my lord,
By your spurning of my society.

KING DARIUS: I left you but a little hour ago.

HAJITHA:

I talk not of my body but of my mind.

KING DARIUS: Hajitha...

HAJITHA:

I'm here, always here for you – but I'm just a flower,
Of use only to perfume your loneliness.

KING DARIUS:

Oh, my queen, will you never understand?
There are regions in a king's meditations,
Wide fields of wanderings and perturbations,

Daniel

Where none but the king may turn to visit.

HAJITHA: None?

KING DARIUS: None.

HAJITHA: No one, my king?

KING DARIUS: No one, my queen.

HAJITHA: Not even Daniel?

KING DARIUS: Ah ... Daniel...

HAJITHA:
I have seen you thirst for talk with Daniel,
Have seen you pine for sweet congress with him.
Together, arm in arm, you have scoured the king's fields,
The perturbed regions of his meditations.
In Daniel's company, my king, you're not lonely.

KING DARIUS: It is different.

HAJITHA: Ah ... it is different.
With Daniel he shares his innermost thoughts,
With his wife and queen only her perfume.

KING DARIUS: Not true at all, Hajitha.
I have shared with you sundry state secrets,
Things no ear should hear till they are well birthed –
Does Daniel know, my queen, my plans for him?
Does any know Daniel shall be chief minister?
Not Daniel, nor any, but you, my queen –
My little flower whose scent perfumes me
To wild and whimsy uxoriousness
And plucks my thoughts ere they are safely ripe.

HAJITHA:
When does Daniel become chief minister?

KING DARIUS:
I shall greet him with the news this very day.

HAJITHA: He returns today then?

KING DARIUS:
So hint letters informing of his success.
Today he comes, hears the news, repairs till
  tomorrow,
Then comes with a decree drafted accordingly,
To be signed and sealed and proclaimed
  empire-wide.
[*Bang at portals.*]
Come!
[*Enter* ZABAK.]

ZABAK: Lord Daniel!

KING DARIUS: Daniel? Daniel!
He comes upon the speaking of his name
Like a true and worthy son of his father!
Let him come! Let him come!
[*Exit* ZABAK. *Enter* DANIEL.]

DANIEL [*bowing*]: Live for ever, O king!

Live for ever, Darius King of Babylon!

KING DARIUS: Daniel!
Come let my arms have you in happy embrace!

DANIEL:
The dust of my rough and rugged travel
Holds my frame from the king's gracious embrace,
But not my heart, which wraps him with happy love.

KING DARIUS:
Has not your house seen you then?

DANIEL:
No, my king; your summons waylaid me afar
And I swerved chariot for the king's palace.

KING DARIUS:
Daniel! My summons was a happy summons
Urgent only with the haste of gladness.
But we must refresh you. Zabak! Fill the cups!
Daniel, sit, sit; let me see you relax.

Zabak! Zabak!

[*Enter* ZABAK *with wine.*]

Yes, Zabak, give us happy cups and gladness.

DANIEL [*making sure, as* ZABAK *prepares to serve him*]: Zabak, water?

ZABAK [*serving him water*]:

I know my lord, and know his ways are constant.

KING DARIUS:

No, Daniel, today call it not water,

For this day is a day of great joys;

Dress it in colored robes and call it wine.

As for my cup, Zabak, give it true grape color.

[ZABAK *leaves after serving* KING DARIUS.]

So, Daniel, is it just as your letters said:

The matter is quelled and put to happy rest?

DANIEL:

Indeed, my king, indeed: For all parties

A most satisfactory end, and all fractures healed.

At first it was all askew, most out of joint,

And then suddenly, to my great surprise –

KING DARIUS:
But not mine, Daniel. You were there in person,
And I have found that when Daniel is there
Every disjoint mends and all fractures heal.
Ah, Daniel! Daniel, my friend and brother!
So sorely have I missed your company!

HAJITHA [*moving away from her obscure corner, mimicking*]:
Ah, Daniel! Daniel, my friend and brother!
So sorely have I missed your company!

DANIEL [*bowing*]: Live for ever, O queen!

HAJITHA:
Has the pale flower in the drab corner
Now become worthy of Daniel's notice?

DANIEL: O queen, live for ever.

HAJITHA [*in mockery*]:
And I have found that when Daniel is there
Every disjoint mends and all fractures heal.
[*She leaves in a huff.*]

KING DARIUS: It runs not deep, Daniel.

DANIEL: What, my lord?

KING DARIUS:
Her jealousy. It's the plague of youth
And youthful ways in women: it works itself out
With puerile whimpers and feline acts of temper.

DANIEL: I am but the king's servant.

KING DARIUS:
And companion, too, in the wanderings of my mind.
It grates her, for she would walk with me where you walk
And delve into the regions of state affairs;
And when I say to her, 'Come not this close,

Your frame may not bear such heavy weight,
Here may men of men, kings and monarchs, only,
    walk,'
She turns and says to me, 'There does Daniel walk.
Is Daniel king?' [*Chuckles.*]
[*Pause.*]
Daniel...

DANIEL: My lord...

KING DARIUS: Would you be king?
[*Pause.*]
Ah, you understand me not.
[*Slight pause.*]
Daniel...

DANIEL: My lord?

KING DARIUS:
Would you be, Daniel, as the king?

DANIEL: As the king, my lord?

Daniel

KING DARIUS:

I've found in you an excellent spirit, Daniel.
In all your undertakings you have excelled.
When first I gleaned your ability
I set you with Satala and Nimri –
Two men I deemed of foremost prowess.
I set you with two to govern my kingdom:
You did, and most excellently; but they misruled.
And even had they ruled, all their ruling,
Set by your governance would have been as a
   firefly's glow
Set by the light of the night's brightest star.
I therefore this day place you over my kingdom,
Over Babylon and my entire empire,
To govern all men on my behalf
As though you yourself were king and monarch.
And so may I, happy in the knowledge
That one of greater ability than I
Was working on my behalf, for my benefit,
Retire to the frolicsome and scented arms
Of a young wife, freed, like no king before me,
From responsibilities of state,

But enjoying all privileges and pleasures,
If so I choose, of a monarch unmatched
In power and eminence since the world began.
Go, Daniel, enjoy the welcome of your house, rest,
And have drafted a decree as I have spoken –
Your first duty as the land's chief minister.

DANIEL: My lord and king...

KING DARIUS:
Yes, Daniel, my lord chief minister, go now; go...
There are moments and times which bear not words,
When emotion must be vesseled tight in silence.
Go now...

DANIEL [*going*]:
Long live the king! Long live King Darius the Mede!

KING DARIUS [*stopping him*]: Ah, Daniel...

DANIEL: My king?

Daniel

KING DARIUS:

I signed today a decree into law
Forbidding any man for the space of thirty days
From bowing in petition and supplication
To any god or man, save to me Darius.
[*Pause.*]

DANIEL: None may bow in prayer to God?

KING DARIUS [*turning away*]:
'Twas the foundling of Satala and Nimri,
Your erstwhile colleagues, now your servants –
Some little symbol, their way of honoring me,
Though I had much rather been honored by good deeds
And proper conduct in office and rule.
Men of improper deeds set great store by symbols,
And by a parade of honors and ceremonies
Seek to divert the eye from their ill ways.
But I know you know what to do with those two.
Now go, Daniel, rest, and then rise to your tasks,
And with the decree be here tomorrow.

[DANIEL *remains rooted to the spot*. KING DARIUS *turns and sees him.*]

Daniel...! Go!

DANIEL [*cracked voice*]:
Live for ever, O king! Live for ever!

[*Exit.*

[*Enter* HAJITHA.]

HAJITHA: What grieves your brother so?

KING DARIUS: My brother?

HAJITHA: Daniel.
Never since heaven kissed mine eyes with light
Has brow or mortal countenance passed me by
Gnarled and furrowed with such fine perplexity.

KING DARIUS:
You, too, would know fine perplexity, Hajitha,
If you were struck, like him, in quick succession
By two great and overwhelming surprises.

Daniel

HAJITHA: Two?

KING DARIUS: His elevation to chief minister –

HAJITHA: That I know of.

KING DARIUS:
And my honoring to something more than king.
Hajitha, men have chosen, from this day,
For the span of thirty days, to honor me.

HAJITHA: To honor you...
Had my king been lacking in honor?

KING DARIUS: To honor me, Hajitha, as a god.

HAJITHA: As a god...

KING DARIUS:
None will bow in prayer or supplication
Through thirty days, to any god or man,
Save to me Darius King of Babylon.

HAJITHA:

But no man has ever been thus honored –

KING DARIUS:

I am Darius the Mede, Conqueror of Babylon, Humiliator of Chaldea and its gods.

HAJITHA: Never before...

KING DARIUS: I am Darius.

HAJITHA:

Yes, my king, and I, more than any, know it.

KING DARIUS:

It is a worthy honor, though quite unsought.

HAJITHA: More an honor
For that reason, my king; more an honor.

KING DARIUS: For thirty days...

Daniel

HAJITHA: A most great honor.

KING DARIUS:
It wore uneasy on me at first,
And so I held my lips till now from saying aught;
But I have grown in the wearing of it
To like it like a robe of finest gold.

HAJITHA:
For so long had you deserved this robe of gold.

KING DARIUS:
It wears well, Hajitha; I like it well.

HAJITHA:
And whose thinking mind spun this golden robe?

KING DARIUS:
Oh, all the chief men of the kingdom. All –
The prefects and satraps and governors...
All the men, my entire kingdom, the world!

HAJITHA:

Though the crowd may take a thought, if it be great,
And swell it, and give it sound and fire,
'Tis often the quiet child of one thinking mind.

KING DARIUS: What matters if it be Satala's?

HAJITHA: Satala's?

KING DARIUS: Or Nimri's?

HAJITHA: Nimri's?

KING DARIUS:
What matters whose child it is – the world approves!

HAJITHA: Does Daniel?

KING DARIUS:
Daniel? But of course! You saw his face –

HAJITHA:
What I saw was a look of perplexity,
Wrought not by joy but by a troubled spirit.

KING DARIUS:
You read not his face keenly then.

HAJITHA:
That man approves not of the king's honoring.

KING DARIUS:
What nonsense! Why would not he approve?

HAJITHA: He is Daniel.

KING DARIUS: And what does that mean?

HAJITHA:
Daniel rejoices not where other men rejoice.
Do you not know your Daniel? He is of strange breed.
He walks not the path of other men, follows none.

If a thing be good but be not of his birthing,
If sound counsel should come from other than his
    lips,
If a plan approved by men be not his,
Daniel turns his back and snorts out stern contempt.
'Tis the way of arrogance, the haughty heart.

KING DARIUS:
I have found him a most worthy statesman.

HAJITHA:
Yes, my king, in matters of his own proposing;
He proposes well and plenty, I grudge not that,
But there lives not the man lord of all wisdom
And all that man may honorably propose.

KING DARIUS:
I vouch that Daniel approves of this my honoring,
Though it be not the offspring of his mind.

HAJITHA:
Mark the words of perspicacity, O king,

Daniel

Remember that your wife and queen said it:
Daniel will fight this thing, with mask or open face.
[*Bang at portals.*]

KING DARIUS: What!

ZABAK [*offstage*]:
Lords Satala and Nimri, O king!
On urgent business!

KING DARIUS: Admit!
[*Enter* SATALA *and* NIMRI.]

SATALA & **NIMRI** [*bowing*]:
Live for ever, O king!
Live for ever, Darius King of Babylon!

KING DARIUS: State your urgent business.
[SATALA *and* NIMRI *are slow to rise.*]
Will you not rise?
[*They rise but are silent.*]
Will you not speak? What madness gathers here?

SATALA: O king...

KING DARIUS: Speak!

SATALA: O king...

KING DARIUS: Speak!

SATALA: Daniel...

KING DARIUS: Daniel?

SATALA: Daniel ... O king...

KING DARIUS: Is Daniel ... d-dead?

NIMRI: He is as good as dead.

SATALA: Unless the king is quick to act!

KING DARIUS: What talk is this?

Daniel

SATALA: The king must act quick!

KING DARIUS: What hunchback talk is this?

SATALA:
A crowd approaches the king's palace –
Jealous with fire for the king's honor!

NIMRI: They cry for Daniel's head!

SATALA:
The king must act quick, if he would save Daniel!

KING DARIUS: What has Daniel done?

SATALA: What has Daniel done?

KING DARIUS: What has Daniel done!

SATALA: Daniel, my king?

KING DARIUS: Daniel! Daniel!

NIMRI: Daniel, my king, is – done for!

SATALA:
Daniel, my king ... Oh ... Oh ... Daniel ... Daniel...

KING DARIUS: Speak! Speak!

SATALA: Nimri, tell the king.

NIMRI:
You have words, Satala, and a quick tongue;
Nimri has only rage, and a swift blade!

KING DARIUS:
Find your quick tongue, Satala, and quickly!
Lest I swiftly find Nimri's rage – and blade!

SATALA: O king ... O king...

KING DARIUS: Speak now!

Daniel

SATALA:
O king, even ... Even, O king ... even...

KING DARIUS: Even?

SATALA: Even, O king, even...

KING DARIUS: Even ... madness...

SATALA: My king ... even ... even...

KING DARIUS [*in high rage now*]: Satala! Satala!

SATALA [*quickly*]: Even, O king, even...
Even as criers cried the city hoarse,
      Even, O king, even...
Even as one such crier stood by Daniel's door
And with gusty power and clear-toned urgency
Cried to all the world the king's new decree,
      Even, O king, even...
Even as men stood by Daniel's front door
And read from a copy stuck there the king's

command,
Even as the world below Daniel's window
Looked up and watched with disbelieving eyes,
Daniel ... O Daniel...

KING DARIUS: What did Daniel do?

SATALA: What did he do, O king?

KING DARIUS: What did he do!

SATALA:
Daniel ... Oh ... Oh ... Daniel has seized my tongue...

KING DARIUS: Daniel seized your tongue?

SATALA:
His act, O king, his act, his very conduct,
His deed, the thing that was his doing –

NIMRI: And very undoing!

Daniel

SATALA:

Speak and tell the king Daniel's deed, Nimri,
Words, my very power, have become the death of
   me.

KING DARIUS: Satala, you speak! Now!

SATALA: O king...
Even as the world below Daniel's window
Looked up and watched with disbelieving eyes,
Daniel threw open his windows and – and –

KING DARIUS: And what did he do?

SATALA: He flung abroad his windows and – and –

NIMRI:

And glad for the curious observing world,
Happy for the eyes that watched in stunned dismay,
Exultant in ignominious defiance,
Daniel stretched forth his hand and – slapped the
   king!

KING DARIUS: He what?

NIMRI:
With impunity, O king! With impunity!

SATALA:
Daniel, before a thousand watching eyes,
Bowed and bent his frame to the very floor,
And with a voice loud as defiant thunder,
Petitioned and made supplication to his God!

NIMRI:
Hear, O king; hear well, great and revered king–

SATALA:
Daniel, before a thousand watching eyes…

NIMRI:
Bowed and bent his frame to the very floor…

SATALA:
And with a voice loud as defiant thunder…

Daniel

NIMRI:

Petitioned and made supplication to his God!

HAJITHA: This cannot be true...

KING DARIUS: Satala...

HAJITHA: O king, it cannot be true!

KING DARIUS:

Satala, what is this thing you front me with?

HAJITHA: It cannot be true!
Not even Daniel would dare do this, O king!

KING DARIUS:

Nimri, what is this thing you say?

HAJITHA:

I said he would fight it, but surely – not this?

[*A clamor is heard offstage. Bang at portals and ZABAK enters.*]

ZABAK:

A rage of the king's officials, my lord!
They bear riotous report to the king
And breathe deadly fire against Lord Daniel!

KING DARIUS [*rising*]: What madness is this?
What lunacy has swooped on the king's court?
[*To* ZABAK, *going*]
 Send for Daniel! A swift and winged chariot!
[*Exits, with* ZABAK.
[*Offstage*] Where are the men, Zabak?
Where are the clamorous mad! Ho there! Satala,
 Nimri!

SATALA & NIMRI: O king!

KING DARIUS [*offstage*]: Who would go
To hasten Daniel here: a sure escort!

SATALA [*to* NIMRI]: Go! Go!
[*Exit* NIMRI.]

Daniel

KING DARIUS [*offstage*]:

A winged chariot! Flying summons! Go, Nimri!

[*His voice recedes as of one going off with the escorts.*]

Speed Daniel here! Race him to me! Away! Away!

Let the chariots fly! Burn the dust with speed!

Let the horses spew fire! Away! Away!

[SATALA *and* HAJITHA, *alone, embrace furtively.*]

HAJITHA: It is almost done.

SATALA: It is just as you said.

HAJITHA: It is always as I say.

SATALA: He suspects not a thing.

HAJITHA: Daniel is dead.

SATALA: Do we meet tonight?

HAJITHA: Yes.

SATALA: Where?

HAJITHA: Here.

SATALA:
Smoothly, so smoothly spins the web of your plan.

HAJITHA:
Smoothly, so smoothly spins the web
Of all the threads of my conjuring.

SATALA: It's done.

HAJITHA: Almost.

SATALA: It will be done.

HAJITHA:
Yes. It will be done. To the very den.

SATALA: I love you.

Daniel

HAJITHA: No.

SATALA: I do.

HAJITHA: Says who?

SATALA: Says me.

HAJITHA: No. Says ambition. And your lust.

SATALA:
Lust fears nothing, respects naught but purity,
And so flees the breadth and radius of my breast;
As for ambition – never did so malignant a monster
Die so quick a death, as when in friendship
You hinted to me of something more and thus bore
The child of all my yearnings, Contentment's scion.
For what lives of note outside my queen's embrace?
[*Hearing* KING DARIUS'S *approach*]
But here comes Folly's true scion...
[*They disengage.*]

KING DARIUS [*offstage, in rising volume*]:
Should a king believe everything he hears?
Madness confers! A gathering of lunacy!
Should men believe all their lunatic eyes tell?
Those men have yielded to insanity;
Lunacy has overtaken them – madness!
Let Daniel come – to speak and explain all!
I'll speak to them no more! Zabak! Strengthen the guards!
Let any break the peace at peril of his life!
[*He enters.*]

SATALA: Live for ever, O king!

KING DARIUS:
Should a king believe everything he hears?
Do ears not mishear? Do eyes not deceive?
Does not the mind see oft with jaundiced eye?
Do men not lie, does not untruth fawn on men,
Do conspirators not witness falsely?
'Tis a babe of a king who believes all reports
That wend their way to the portals of his ears!

Daniel

I'll have Daniel here to give this lie its due!

HAJITHA:
The king knows what little love I bear Daniel;
And it was but a little while ago I said:
'Daniel will fight this thing with mask or open face,'
Yet, like the king, I cannot bring myself
To believe that Daniel would do as they have said,
And choose so dishonorable a revenge.
No, my king, Daniel would not do as they have said.

KING DARIUS: Satala, I fear for your life.

SATALA: My life, O king?

KING DARIUS: Death stalks not afar.

SATALA: For whom, O king?

KING DARIUS: Death crouches at the door.

SATALA:

'Tis Daniel, not I, who dishonored the king.

KING DARIUS:

Death comes soon for you, Satala. It will not miss.

SATALA:

Daniel dishonored the king, not I.

KING DARIUS: You lie!

SATALA:

Would it were so, my lord, and craven falsehood,
For I love Daniel and will not see him die.
[*Silence.* KING DARIUS *paces.*]

HAJITHA: Why does the king pace?

KING DARIUS [*stopping*]:
'Tis but the lies of men –
The wicked invention of vile malice.

Daniel

HAJITHA:
I vouch 'tis as the king says, for Daniel,
Though a man filled with pride and great self-will,
Has much good in him, and though perhaps envious now
Of the success of another's conception,
Would not let spite so overthrow his good sense,
To plot the king such dastard dishonor.

KING DARIUS [*pacing again*]:
'Tis but the falsehood of conspiracy –
The scheme of men who nurse Daniel marvelous ill.

HAJITHA:
Let the king then have no worry. Sit, my king.
I beg your majesty, may it please the king sit?
[KING DARIUS *sits. Silence.* KING DARIUS *rises and paces again.*]
The king worries. Why does the king worry?
Here, my king, some wine. Will not my lord have wine?
Oh, my poor dear husband worries, he worries.
The king loves his servant, yet has no faith in him;

I love not Daniel, yet have much faith in him:
I know what he will do, and what not do.
Would the king were half as trusting as I.
Here, Satala, cool your palate with wine,
Ere Daniel comes and days of wine perish.
[*Bang at portals.*]

KING DARIUS: Come!
[*Enter* ZABAK.]

ZABAK: My king –

KING DARIUS: Where is Daniel!

ZABAK:
The escorts are hard on the way, I'm sure, my king.

KING DARIUS:
Why do the chariots delight in delay?
Why does time ever drag when haste summons?
Why does it tramp and trudge with shortish legs?

Daniel

ZABAK: My king,
A new murmur of city officials have come,
Dogged by a mob with brutish tempers.

KING DARIUS: What have they come for?

ZABAK:
They bear a report of Lord Daniel
In vein and fractious manner of the last.

KING DARIUS:
I'll not hear it! I'll see no one! I'll see none
Till Daniel comes and from his lips hear all!
My command stands: they breach the peace and die!
Who touches one strand of Daniel's hair dies!
Prop the guards to riot stemming! Go, Zabak!
Hold back no lance! They breach the peace and die!
[*Exit* ZABAK. *Noise and bustle offstage.*]
What commotion is that? Has Daniel come?

ZABAK [*offstage, shouting*]:
Lord Nimri with Lord Daniel!

KING DARIUS [*in a riot of emotions*]:
Daniel...! Daniel...! Daniel...!
[*Enter* NIMRI *with* DANIEL.]
Daniel...
[*Long pause.*]

DANIEL [*subdued voice*]:
Live for ever, O king.
Live for ever, Darius King of Babylon.

KING DARIUS: Daniel...
[*Pause.*]

DANIEL: My king?

KING DARIUS: Tell me it is not so...

DANIEL: What, my king?

KING DARIUS: I have received reports...
[*Pause.*]

Daniel

DANIEL: What reports, my king?

KING DARIUS:
Then it is not so; I knew it! I knew it!
I knew, Daniel, that these men spoke malice.
Satala! Nimri! Death crouches for you!

SATALA: We spoke not false, my king.

NIMRI: Ask Daniel, O king.

KING DARIUS:
Daniel knows not of the report you bear!

NIMRI: Ask him, O king.

SATALA:
Indeed, my lord, the man stands before the king;
Will it not please his majesty ask him?

KING DARIUS:
What manner of malice mates before me?

Since when did cobra spite come to Babylon?

SATALA [*prostrating*]:
Ask him, my lord, ask him.

NIMRI [*stiff shouldered*]:
Ask him, O king, ask him!

HAJITHA:
They speak with lips slobbering heavy with slander;
Daniel would never wreak the king such dishonor!

SATALA:
Outside the people clamor for his head;
Will not abide so damned a deed against the king –

NIMRI:
The man himself will scarce deny the deed!

SATALA: As I love Daniel,
And will die ere I see Daniel perish,
I urge the king to act with utmost speed,

Daniel

Lest the will of the people wedge him tight,
And their rage, towering bloody at Daniel's offense,
Should force the king's hand to the doom of a dear
  friend.

NIMRI [*to* SATALA]: It is the law of the Medes:
The king's decree, once sealed, may not be revoked.

SATALA: Nevertheless...

NIMRI:
You intercede in vain; your dear friend is dead.

SATALA: He must not die.

KING DARIUS:
Must I gawk and watch lunacy disport?

HAJITHA:
Daniel, did you do this thing accusation bares?
[*Quickly*] See, his face lights up with innocence!
Daniel is falsely accused! Wickedly maliced!

Daniel who loved the king above all men,
Daniel whom the king loved as brother and friend –
Even as father, seeing him filled with ancient
   wisdom
And antique love, is not so unwise, so treacherous,
So betraying, so callous and heartless,
So ignoble and perfidious, so wicked –
So wicked! – So wicked and so base,
As to stretch an evil leg and trip the king,
Strip him screaming naked before the world,
Feed him with grass to eat and sand to snaffle on,
Rub his eyes with hot and stinging pepper,
Immerse his head in the slime and dunghill
Of abject dishonor, and call him bastard!

KING DARIUS:
Trim your flame, Hajitha; Daniel is not that man!

HAJITHA:
Then why abide these men any longer?
Dispatch them to the death they wished Daniel!
Send them to the den; cast them to the lions!

Daniel

KING DARIUS: The report is false, Daniel –
Say it so and see these men to a bloody death.

SATALA [*almost simultaneously with* NIMRI *and* HAJITHA *below*]:
He will not deny it –

NIMRI: A world of witnesses bear us out –

HAJITHA: Arrant falsehood –

KING DARIUS:
Silence! Let Daniel speak! Let all be silent!
[*Silence.*]
The report is false, Daniel? Say it so.

DANIEL:
I know not what report the king speaks of,
Or what accusation these men bring against me,
Nor for what matter the queen, so assiduously,
So ably, appears to defend me.
[*Long silence.*]

KING DARIUS: Daniel...

DANIEL: My king...

KING DARIUS:
Were you in the king's presence earlier this day?

DANIEL: Yes, my king.

KING DARIUS:
Did the king inform you of the passing
Of a new decree forbidding any man
For thirty days to bow in prayer
To any man or god, save to the king?

DANIEL: Yes, my king.
[*Pause.*]

KING DARIUS:
Did you then go home to bow to your God?

DANIEL: Yes, my king.

Daniel

[*Utter silence. Long pause.*]

KING DARIUS: Why?
[*Long pause.*]

DANIEL: Because...
[*Pause.*]
He is God.

KING DARIUS: He is God...
[*Pause.*]
Who is God?

DANIEL: God.

KING DARIUS: Your God?

DANIEL:
My God, and your God, the God of the earth,
And the God of the heavens, our Maker,
The God of all creation, of all that is.
[*Pause.*]

KING DARIUS: Daniel...

DANIEL: My king...

KING DARIUS: Am I your king?

DANIEL: You are my king.

KING DARIUS:
Your king says to you: 'Bow to no one,
Nor man nor god.' But you defy your king
And to your God you bend your frame and bow.
Why?

DANIEL: You are king.
[*Pause.*]
He ... is God.
[*Long pause.*]

KING DARIUS:
To whom do you owe allegiance, your king or God?

DANIEL: To my king.
[*Pause.*]
And my God.
[*Pause.*]

KING DARIUS:
To whom do you owe foremost allegiance?
[*Pause.*]

DANIEL: To my God.
[*Long pause.*]

KING DARIUS: Above me?
[*Pause.*]

DANIEL: Above you.
[*Long pause.*]

KING DARIUS: Satala!

SATALA: My king!

KING DARIUS:

Do you, like Daniel, serve any gods?

SATALA:

Twenty-seven, my king! May I list them?

KING DARIUS:

Beware, Satala! Beware! Should the king's ears
Become pasture for the names of Satala's gods?
Now, Satala! To whom do you owe allegiance?

SATALA:

If the king commanded me slay my gods
I would gladly do it and pull their beards at it!

KING DARIUS: Nimri, how many gods?

NIMRI:

Nothing like Satala's, O king, and for good reason:
I have found gods a rather flawed bunch of idlers,
Acting with less certitude than my arm.
My service therefore is given to two only –

Daniel

And that with sham and mocking allegiance.

KING DARIUS: Hajitha?

HAJITHA:
My love makes my husband, the king, my god.
[*Pause.*]

KING DARIUS:
The allegiance of your co-subjects –
You have heard them, Daniel; what have you to say?

DANIEL:
They speak thus who serve false gods, and know not
 God.
My words balk to keep company with theirs –
Which brim with ripe and fatal ignorance!

HAJITHA: Hear Lord Pride himself speak!

KING DARIUS: Silence!
[*Pause.*]

I have fed you, Daniel, have loved you richly,
Have made you the envy of men, have made you
    great,
You who are in truth a bondsman, a Hebrew slave...

DANIEL:
And I have served you as men should serve their
    king;
I have loved you more than duty commands me.
I have been a faithful subject and a grateful ward.

KING DARIUS:
Faithful! Grateful! who dishonors me vilely?
[*Pause.*]
And your God – if you must serve a God
And give him allegiance above the king –
Should the world know? Must it be proclaimed
    abroad?
If you must slight the king and belittle him,
Must it be before the gaze of men quick to mock?
Can your God not be worshiped in private?
Cannot he be served in your secret heart?

Daniel

Had you bowed to Him in your shuttered room,
Who would have known, who would have said thus
   did Daniel?

DANIEL:

I serve God, and in the service of God
Lies a testifying before men that God is God –
Above the laws of men and the commands of kings.
To worship God in secret when the season begs
An outward witness of God's supremacy,
Is to annul my servitude and dishonor God.
[*Pause.*]

KING DARIUS:

Will this your God benefit from your death?
Can service to your God be done from your grave?

DANIEL:
There is service in death, if so He wills.

KING DARIUS: You are a fool!
[*Pause.*]

Once I thought you a tower among the wise,
Once I saw you the pride and flower of counsel,
Once, up above, upon the mountain peak
Of high understanding, upon the stars,
The farthest reaches of piercing insight,
You hung your cloak, your cape of shrewdest
    judgment;
Now, down in the valley, in festering bog,
Swamp lands, bad lands, vile and marshy country,
You have spread your mantle, to gather the remains
Of rack and ruin, the fall of shriveled petals.
There, in swamp lands, vile and marshy country,
You tower still, but only in grand folly,
A giant among the imprudent dull.
[*Pause.*]
Daniel, you are a fool!
[*Pause.*]
Are you righteous, Daniel? Dare he make such boast
Who breaks the law with unrepentant abandon?

DANIEL:
When man's edict conflicts with God's canon,

Daniel

When the command of kings affronts God's law,
The law of mortal man loses its behest.

KING DARIUS: You speak treason!

DANIEL: I speak divine truth.
[*Long pause.*]
[KING DARIUS *goes to* NIMRI, *who is busy inspecting his knife.*]

KING DARIUS: Nimri.

NIMRI [*gaze unswerving from his blade*]: My king.

KING DARIUS: You wait.

NIMRI: Yes, my king.

KING DARIUS: For what?

NIMRI [*casting a glance at* DANIEL]: For death.

KING DARIUS: For death.

NIMRI [*casting another glance at* DANIEL]:
Yes, my king.

KING DARIUS [*walking away*]:
Nimri waits for death.
[*He goes over to* SATALA, *who has been stalking and hovering around* DANIEL.]
Satala, why do you stalk and prowl around
Like a bloodletting panther, a beast of death?

SATALA [*stopping*]:
A panther? Me, O king? The king knows
I am but a doe's innocent nursling,
A child's sweet pet, gentle in all my ways,
Soft and tender, and slow even to tread ground,
Lest, perchance, I hurt the unwary earth.

KING DARIUS [*turning to* HAJITHA]:
Hajitha, come to me.
[HAJITHA *goes to him.*]
Is that Daniel?

Daniel

HAJITHA [*looking sorrowfully at* DANIEL]:
Once ... he was Daniel.

KING DARIUS:
Hajitha, speak to me. Is this Daniel, the faithful?

HAJITHA:
Once he was Daniel the faithful...
But let not my king hold a thought to it,
Let not my king ponder as monarchs do,
For my king is more than mere monarch,
More than mortal man. Have not all men said so?

KING DARIUS [*looking at* DANIEL]: All men?
[HAJITHA, *silent, triumphant, slinks back to her seat.*]
[*Pause.*]
[KING DARIUS *goes to* NIMRI, *who is still attentive to his blade.*]

KING DARIUS [*gently*]: Nimri...

NIMRI [*still attentive to his blade*]: My king.

KING DARIUS [*suddenly, harsh*]: Hide that blade!

NIMRI [*sheathing it*]: My king.
[*Pause.*]

KING DARIUS [*gently*]: Nimri...

NIMRI: My king.

KING DARIUS [*suddenly stretching out his hand, harsh*]: The blade!

NIMRI [*handing it to him*]: My king.
[KING DARIUS *walks away with the knife.*]

NIMRI [*watching him go*]:
Once, at Ashkenaz, in the black belly
Of midnight's deepest rage, a mere lad,
I found a thousand ways to thrust that blade
And let out blood; warm blood, rich and bubbly.
[*Gesturing at* DANIEL]
That traitor, O king, has veins of rich blood.
Will it not please the king have me show the king,

Daniel

In the belly of that man, my thousand ways?

KING DARIUS: Silence!

[*In a fit he stabs a table with the knife, and leaves it there, embedded, quivering.*]

[*Pause.*]

[*He turns his attention to* SATALA, *who has resumed stalking* DANIEL, *inspecting him near-comically.*]

KING DARIUS:

Satala, why do you hover and scrab around

Like a carrion buzzard, a bird of death?

SATALA [*stopping*]:

A buzzard? Me, O king? The king knows

I am but a dove's younger brother,

A bird of peace, gentle in all my ways,

Soft and tender, and slow even to draw breath,

Lest, perchance, I hurt the delicate air.

[*Pause.*]

KING DARIUS:

See, Daniel, death perches on your shoulder,

It hovers and beats wing above your head,
And I only may command death begone.
Repent, Daniel; repent of your words and take life;
Repent of your defiance, ask pardon,
And take life, riches and honor, great position.
I offer you life, Daniel; embrace life!

NIMRI: The king's decree may not be revoked!

KING DARIUS: Silence! Upon your life, silence!
[*Pause.*]
I am king. I am Darius the Mede.
I growled for Babylon and seized it!
I laid waste the powers of Babylon
And none could stop me! Nor Nimri nor any man!
Though the king's decree, Daniel, may not be
    revoked,
Yet I am king, and the king may do as he wills,
And find means to accomplish his desires.
I offer you life, Daniel; seize it!

Daniel

DANIEL:

Years together, and the king knows not Daniel...

KING DARIUS:

Daniel! Daniel! When will you cast away
This frigid staff of righteousness? Look, Daniel,
The art of life is the art of compromise:
To yield and bend with the wind of expedience,
And slack off in season, and firm up with prudence;
And to give and take and share, or else withhold,
As the times command and good sense will have!

DANIEL:

Compromise? Yield and bend? Expedience?
Beware expedience, O king, it is double-faced,
Of changing gait, and walks not firm with lone-faced truth;
And compromise dines with prudence and good sense
Only where integrity is honored guest.
[*Pause.*]

KING DARIUS:

I who loved you like a favorite brother,
And opened to you the doors of my heart,
And flung in your arms my confidences
As I would to a foremost and trusted friend,
Though you were but a common bondsman, a slave:
You have thrown me in disgrace, obloquy.

DANIEL: Not I, O king.

KING DARIUS: Who?

DANIEL: You yourself.
[*Hush.*]
[KING DARIUS *in head-wagging distress.*]
For you yourself have thought to take the place of
    God.
God is God, and man is man though he be king;
No man is king but God makes him so,
And no man gains worth but God enables.
Therefore must men, king and all, honor God.

Daniel

KING DARIUS:

I know not your God and fear him not,
As you, Daniel, neither fear nor honor your king!

DANIEL:

I fear you, O king, but I fear God more;
And I must speak as God would have me speak.
And though I'm your servant, I'm first God's
    servant,
And must love you, and serve and honor you,
Only as may honor my first allegiance.

KING DARIUS: No more!
Blight my ears no more with your righteous treason!
Zabak! Zabak!

ZABAK [*offstage*]: My king!

KING DARIUS:

Take this man away and feed him to the lions!
And may his God whom he serves above me save
    him!

[ZABAK *enters.*]
[SATALA *and* NIMRI *seize* DANIEL.]

Lights dim.

Darkness.

Act 2

Same place, hours later at night.

Spotlight comes on and illuminates KING DARIUS'S *face, ravaged by grief, staring vacantly at the audience. Spotlight grows. The King takes off his crown, stares at it and puts it aside. Lights grow to reveal that the King is all alone on the stage, but the lights do not brighten beyond night tone. The King paces a while, then moans, cudgels his head with his hands and lets out a great bellow.*

ZABAK *enters alarmed. He sees that it is the sound of grief, and can only stand and watch, and grieve, too, in sympathy. At length he coughs to attract the King's attention.*

ZABAK:

O king, the night is deep-steeped in governance;

Will not the king repair to his chamber

And to the healing balm of sleep's embrace?

[KING DARIUS, *distracted, stumbles to him.*]

KING DARIUS:

I cannot sleep, no. Night comes, and sleep flees.
Why has sleep plucked my peace and fled my
  breast?
Why am I like one bereft of choicest gift?
Who is Daniel? What is the man to me?
Was Daniel sired of my father's loins?
No! More precious by far than such a one was he
Who played the thrice-blessed role of trusted friend,
Able counselor, and most devoted subject.
Here was Daniel, my joy and golden promise
Of brighter tomorrows in silvered age –
And here – here! In the bounds of this very here! –
Were those two unworthies and that woman,
And in the space of a shriveled evening
Daniel is no more...
[*Pause.*]

ZABAK:

Here is no place to be, my king, on such a night;
Your sleeping quarters bear their wonted welcome.

Daniel

KING DARIUS: To bed with you, Zabak.

ZABAK: My king...

KING DARIUS: To bed!

ZABAK [*bowing and leaving*]:
As my king commands.
           [*Exit.*

KING DARIUS [*pacing again*]:
Would you presume to walk my grief's course,
    Zabak?
None but Daniel walked my course or knew my
    path,
And now Daniel is no more...
[*Pause.*]
[*Heartbroken*]
And how he stood like a man before my fire!
Had I heard it told in tale or fable
I'd have held the exploit proud to my breast;
But since the deed affronts my very self,

Like a royal hypocrite, a regal two-face,
I cast the deed from me as sup for beasts.
[*Pause.*]
A blaze of kings arrayed in golden robes
Will not match the shine of Daniel's spirit,
Nor all the armor of war-proud valor
Best the iron-breast of that Jew's courage!
[*Pause.*]
Daniel! Hot did your words burn and deep did they pierce
When you said 'Man is man though he be king':
For I am mere man, the smallest of men,
I who cannot stifle my heart's sobbing,
Nor quench the grief within for what my hand has wrought:
The hand of my pride – Pride, the bane of kings,
And the snare of fools – Fool! – Fool that I am
To deny the existence of a Maker
And say no hand made me, none wrought my form!
No! I'm not so lifted with pride, so sunk in sin
I cannot see, that though I have conquered lands
And trampled the earth with hooves and chariot

Daniel

   wheels,
And with the sweep of my sword and marvelous arm
Have won the homage of nations and men –
That grain of sand, the tiniest in my empire,
That strand of hair, the thinnest in my kingdom –
Defies my arm and power to mold or forge.
[*Pause.*]
Even the secrets that lurk in that woman's eyes,
Those little mysteries that dance in her dark sloes,
Defy my searching out, though I'm not roundly
   fooled:
The little vixen wears mischief about her
Like the quiet hugging of a secret girdle.
I sensed her little witcheries in today's ado
But saw not clearly their substance and form...
[*Laughter is heard offstage, approaching.*]
[KING DARIUS *reacts with surprise. He moves to the door as if to inspect, but on second thoughts retreats to a darkened portion of the chamber. He does not totally conceal himself until the proceedings following progress.*]
[*Enter* HAJITHA *and* SATALA, *engaged in intimacies and unaware of the watching king.*]

HAJITHA:

Let me go, Satala, your grip is hard.

SATALA: I'm a man.

HAJITHA: But I'm a woman...

SATALA:

I could not forget that, my love, though your mind heaves
With the bulging biceps of men that shall be kings.

HAJITHA:

No, it is the mind of a woman who loves,
And loves desperately. Love muddles thinking,
But desperate love sharpens it. Oh, Satala...

SATALA:

And who, my lovely and precious Hajitha,
Is the lucky object of your desperate love?

HAJITHA: One whose love I often doubt.

Daniel

SATALA:
What would you have him do to prove his love?

HAJITHA: Let him hold me with gentle hands.

SATALA: Come then, my precious...

HAJITHA: With gentle hands...

SATALA: Come...

HAJITHA: No ... your grip is hard.

SATALA: Hajitha...

HAJITHA: Come kiss me then.
But tenderly, Satala, not bruisingly.

SATALA:
Sweet the gain unkerneled in the loss
When the king sent not for you tonight.

HAJITHA:

His heart breaks tonight for Daniel.

SATALA: But might not he still send?

HAJITHA:

It's not his way, being so late; but if he does,
Do not my maids know where to find me?
The usual signal on the door and I'm gone.

SATALA: When I am king...

HAJITHA: Yes?

SATALA: When I am king...
I forswear ever to send for you.

HAJITHA: No?

SATALA:

The hand never sends for its fingers,
Nor does the eye search the night for its socket.

Daniel

As in my breast my gentle heart abides
So by my side my tender love belongs...
Ever!

HAJITHA: Oh, Satala...
[*Slight pause.*]

SATALA: Do you love me, Hajitha?

HAJITHA: Do you doubt?

SATALA: Say it. I like to hear it.

HAJITHA: I need not.
For you I sent a man to the lions.

SATALA:
Your plan worked to the tip and finest edge.
I stand in awe of you, Hajitha.

HAJITHA: Stand only in awe of love.

SATALA: And how the king fell for it!

HAJITHA: The blind uxorious fool!
[*A sound as of something heavy falling.*]
[*They start.*]

HAJITHA: Did you hear?

SATALA: Ssh!

HAJITHA: There!

SATALA: Ssh!

HAJITHA: Something lurks there.

SATALA [*inching off*]:
A little investigation, a peep in the dark,
Will do the night no harm nor hurt our gentle senses.

HAJITHA: 'Twas the sound of a falling thing...

SATALA: Yes.

HAJITHA: Or a person...

SATALA [*turning and giving her a sharp look*]: A person?
[*Pause.*]
[*He steals into the dark portion.*]
[*Pause.*]

SATALA [*in the dark*]: Ha!

HAJITHA [*hushed*]: Satala!

SATALA: Be you taken!

HAJITHA: W-what?

SATALA: The king!

HAJITHA: The king? Oh!

SATALA: He's taken!

HAJITHA: The king!

SATALA [*coming out of the dark with a smile, bearing a bust*]: Here is your king.

HAJITHA: The king's bust!

SATALA: It fell...

HAJITHA: Oh...

SATALA: From it's shaky stand...

HAJITHA: I thought it was the king!

SATALA: As the king must fall...

HAJITHA: I thought we were dead!

SATALA: As Darius the king must fall
From his menaced dais when my knife finds his

heart.

HAJITHA: No!

SATALA: It must be!

HAJITHA: No!

SATALA: We agreed!

HAJITHA: Yes, but not you!

SATALA: Who then? You?

HAJITHA: No – Nimri.

SATALA: Nimri?

HAJITHA:
Yes, let Nimri slaughter the king. Not you.

SATALA: Nimri!

HAJITHA:

He is snug and perfect fit for my plan.

SATALA:

That man lacks stealth, has not the slightest artifice!
Is fit only for loud and open slaughters,
Havoc and mayhem, and brazen destructions!

HAJITHA:

And more is he the perfect man for it.
He will serve our ends well – the murderous fool,
And kill the king, with all his bloodied fingers
Pointing to him and screeching loud his guilt.
Satala, I have it wrapped up, trust me.
Now that Daniel, the king's true garrison,
His surest shield, is thrust out of the way,
The king makes Satala chief minister,
And by my artful help Satala grows
In stature and power and appeal,
And at such a time as seems ripe to me,
Nimri slays the king, and the chief minister
Apprehends the assassin and executes him,

Which act increases his appeal,
And enables him take without a murmur
The throne for himself, and his loving queen.

SATALA: Will Nimri do it?

HAJITHA:
He has hopes and ambitions and desires
That will boil the blood in you if you knew.

SATALA:
Nimri desires the throne? And the queen?

HAJITHA:
He's a fool; and like the king and all fools,
He'll be squeezed for his juice and tossed away.

SATALA:
And I thought I, only, hoped to be king.

HAJITHA: You, only, shall be king.

SATALA:

Dare Nimri aspire to such heights?

HAJITHA:

It's the privilege of men to aspire,
And their lot to reap failure's runny end.

SATALA:

Such aspirations make a man dangerous.

HAJITHA: Do you fear him?

SATALA: Fear him?

HAJITHA: Fear him not.

SATALA:

I fear him not; I quail only in marvel
At the wanton profligacy of hope
That makes the housefly crave the eagle's height.

Daniel

HAJITHA:

Have no thought; I know the strings of his harp
As well as the king's and Daniel's, and will play them,
As smoothly as I did the king's and Daniel's,
To give me all the music my heart would have.

SATALA:

Take care, my dove, he's a man of violent ways –

HAJITHA:

And violent greed, which besetting fault,
Played with mastery, will give me sweet music,
As the king's pride does, and Daniel's reverence did.
But go, my love, the night soon sheds its coat,
And we must be here to play the king again.

SATALA: A little sleep and I'll be ready.

HAJITHA:

Sleep is a luxury when men would be kings;
Have none. We must attend the king ere Nimri

comes.

SATALA: Will Nimri come?

HAJITHA:
If I read the skies as well as I play the harp,
Nimri's greed will kill sleep and bring him here.
He, like us, would think to play the king's heart –
Stripped tender by grief from loss of Daniel
And the peeling power of early morn –
He would think, like us, to press the king
And wrest from him the post of chief minister.
But go, my love, that the morning may hasten here
And give ambition one further fillip
On the steady road to happy success.

SATALA [*kissing her*]:
My love, and the flame of my desires...
[*Exit.*

HAJITHA [*laughing*]:
What fools men are! Of cheap and little use

Daniel

But as toys and playthings to be dangled
By scheming maids or clever matrons
On little mocking strings, and perchance played
As one may a tried lute or mastered harp.
They look far but see little beyond their nose,
For pride, like a dark veil, falls from their brow
And drapes off any seeing but what pride allows:
They look a woman's way and see not her substance
But the picture foist by vanity's conceit:
A useful dollop of obedient flesh
Molded for the pleasure of lustful loins,
The feeding of dilated egos,
Or the vapid chore of baby breeding.
[*Pause.*]
Some hold them as fit only to be spurned –
As did Daniel. Yes, Daniel, you spurned me.
I gave you my heart but you had no eyes:
I was nothing to you but a little fly
Disturbing the gaze of your noble face.
Ask now for Daniel ... Where is Daniel?
Daniel, where are you? Prince, noble and damned!
You stood by your God and by your God you fell,

Stung by a little fly for whom you had no face.
Ah, proud Daniel! Too proud to stoop to sin.
Your pride, though of different face, was one with
    the king's,
For pride is pride, and all pride is folly,
And destruction dogs ever the heels of the fool.
[*Pause.*]
Pride has lost the king his garrison in Daniel
And pride will lose the king his very life;
For a serpent coils beneath his pillow
And must sting him to uncoil to greatness,
But vanity shows the king the flower only
That scents his pillow, not the serpent.
[*Laughing*]
Satala, you too! Prince of little fools!
You share the common folly of the king's court!
So you would be king? Satala, you?
No, Satala, I, Hajitha, shall be monarch:
Ruler of all Babylon, empress of the earth,
The pride of ages! The flower of centuries!
And by my star, the stars of Sheba and Nefertiti
Shall be as the twinkle of the king's dying tears.

Daniel

[*Laughing and leaving*]
What fools men are! What silly little fools!
[*Exit.*
[KING DARIUS *emerges in palpable anguish. He moans, then pulls off his wedding ring.*]

KING DARIUS:
This gold of love was naught but hidden beast,
A serpent that now uncoils in stinging hiss.
[*He hurls the ring away.*]
Begone from me, vile hissing beast! Begone!
[*He paces in implacable wrath.*]
Cobra top and wicked hood of deceit –
Filled with viperous evil and aspic works!
The pith and pulse of perfect perversity!
[*Pause.*]
Daniel! O Daniel!
In darkest night does your star shine brighter still!
Would that the God whom you feared and dreaded
Above the fear and dread of kings and death,
Had in his dreadful arm the strong power
To snatch life from death and revive dead bones,
And give again to his faithful servant

The gift of breath, to his obedient one,

The lease again of life, and bring you back

To a grieving king, a wretched monarch!

[*He falls to his knees, overcome by the weight of monumental pain.*]

[*Pause.*]

[*Lights fail for a while, then come on gradually, growing stronger than before to signify dawn.*]

Dawn rises to meet the day and light breaks forth,

But lightens not the night of my wretched heart!

[*Enter ZABAK.*]

[*Oblivious of* KING DARIUS'S *presence, he yawns and stretches and proceeds to do some tidying up.*]

KING DARIUS: Zabak...

ZABAK [*starting*]: My king!

[*He collects himself and bows.*]

Live for ever, O king!

Live for ever, Darius King of Babylon!

KING DARIUS:

You have come with the dawn, on the wings of light:

Daniel

Would you had come with the light of Daniel!

ZABAK:

Did my king remain here the livelong night?
[*Silence.*]

KING DARIUS: Zabak...

ZABAK: My king?

KING DARIUS:
Send to the lions' den for Daniel.

ZABAK: Send for Daniel?

KING DARIUS:
Send for what remains of him, his robe
In bloody strips, a sandal or a ring,
An anklet that defied the lions' teeth –
Let me have aught that remains of Daniel
That I may sink it in this sad breast,
And by its property hold my breaking heart.

ZABAK:

Let my king not send thus, whose end is naught
But blood and death's stench, and sorrowing sorrow.

KING DARIUS:

Send as I say, Zabak. I have spoken.

ZABAK [*bowing*]:

My king is king, his word is done.

[*Exit.*]

[*Enter* HAJITHA.]

HAJITHA:

My king is up early, or did my king not sleep?
Oh, poor husband, your face is drawn,
Pulled taut with the world's cares.
[*She rubs his cheek tenderly.*]
I waited for you all of last night, dear husband;
You sent not for me.

KING DARIUS:

This last night that passed was not the night of love.

Daniel

HAJITHA:

If the king's heart is heavy, should I, his wife,
His queen, his scented flower, not, upon his bed,
Give him my breasts to pour thereon his soul,
And thus ease his cares, or, perchance, erase them?

KING DARIUS: I lay not upon my bed last night.

HAJITHA:

Then would I have paced the king's chamber with
   the king,
And with words' sweetness, born not of mere will,
But by my great love, have chased off his sorrows.

KING DARIUS:

I paced not my chamber last night; I was not there.

HAJITHA:

Where was my king then?

KING DARIUS: In a place
Where knowledge visited and understanding came.

HAJITHA: Where?

KING DARIUS:

In the playground of sweet and bitter dawning
Where light is dark, and dark is light and bright.

HAJITHA: Where, O king?
[*Silence.*]
[*The King goes to* NIMRI'S *knife of the preceding day, still embedded in the table, and tugs it out. He inspects it menacingly.*]
The king's words
Are puzzling, and his silence mystifying.

KING DARIUS:

Not as mystifying as dragon ambition in a butterfly.

HAJITHA: Dragon ambition in a butterfly?

KING DARIUS:

Dragon ambition, whose hatching and escape
Will infest the air with teeming scorpions,
And give havoc new teeth, and death fresh sting!

Daniel

[*He drives the knife into the table as before.*]

HAJITHA:

The king's words bend and twist me out of form
And lose me in labyrinthine byways.
Is it Daniel? It is Daniel – I know it!
Daniel come from the dead to plague the king.
Forget him! Forget his deed! Forget all!
You have revenged yourself, what more remains?
Why should the king mourn a betrayal avenged?
Forget your hurts, O king! Forget the slight,
Forget the past, and move on to greet the future:
Which augurs well, for Treachery was cut off early,
Ere he acquired the robe of chief minister
To do the king a train of greater dishonors.
And on the subject of chief minister...
My king, do you not think that Satala –

KING DARIUS: Thus does the serpent uncoil...

HAJITHA: My king?

KING DARIUS: The hiss of the serpent...

HAJITHA: I understand not the king.

KING DARIUS: Ere the serpent strikes...

HAJITHA: Perhaps my lord needs some rest?

KING DARIUS: Such rest as I need I cannot have while the serpent draws breath.

HAJITHA: My lord, I fear for your health.
[KING DARIUS *walks to her and stares into her face.*]

KING DARIUS: See the serpent.

HAJITHA: My lord?

KING DARIUS [*suddenly, violently, pointing at the floor by her feet*]: See the serpent!
[HAJITHA *jumps with fright, eyes looking out for the serpent.*]

HAJITHA: Oh! What a fright
The king gave me; it is but a ring.

KING DARIUS: Pick it up!

HAJITHA [*picking it*]: It's the king's ring.

KING DARIUS: Which of the king's rings?

HAJITHA: My lord speaks so strangely;
His ways today mystify and frighten me.

KING DARIUS: Answer!

HAJITHA: Why my lord,
It's the king's band of matrimony.

KING DARIUS:
The coil of treachery! The serpent's symbol! –
When sloe-eyed deceit acts the lamb of love.
[*Bang at portals.*]
Come!

[*Enter* ZABAK.]

ZABAK: Lord Satala, my king.

KING DARIUS: Admit!
[*As* ZABAK *is going*] Zabak!

ZABAK [*stopping*]: My king?

KING DARIUS:
Where are they, whom I sent for Daniel:
To fetch the remains of royal folly?

ZABAK:
They hasten here, I'm sure, my lord.

KING DARIUS: Stand not on ceremony;
Admit them as they come, true lightbearers.

ZABAK [*bowing*]: My king.
[*Exit.*
[*Enter* SATALA.]

SATALA: Live for ever, O king!

KING DARIUS: How is this to be?

SATALA: My king?

KING DARIUS:
Can he live who men conspire to slay?

SATALA: I understand you not, my king.

KING DARIUS:
Men whispered for Daniel's life and he died;
Will the king live, whom whispers, too, have marked?

SATALA [*casting a fearful glance at* HAJITHA]:
The king speaks obscure.

KING DARIUS: So the serpent has said.
How fared your night's escapades, Satala?

SATALA: What escapades, my king?

KING DARIUS:
Where were you last night, Satala?

SATALA: The king speaks strangely –

KING DARIUS: Where!

SATALA:
Where? Why, my king, where but upon my bed!

KING DARIUS: Mistressed?

SATALA: My king?

KING DARIUS:
Where you mistressed last night, Satala?

SATALA: My king!

KING DARIUS: Answer!

Daniel

SATALA: My king knows I'm well-wived!

KING DARIUS: Well-wived!
Deceived are many who think themselves
 well-wived.
Perfidy! How you wrap the world with iron arms!
[*Pause.*]
Oh, Daniel! Oh...

SATALA:
Oh, it's Daniel? His treachery is paid for, O king!
With these eyes I saw him cast to the lions;
I saw the stone rolled on to seal the den;
With these ears did I hear the pounce of beasts,
The rumble of mighty beasts, raging beasts,
And then a silence, the silence of death.
Daniel is no more, his treachery paid for.

KING DARIUS:
You heard the beasts? I saw the beast, and see him
 still.
And the serpent, too. Here is the beast;

And here is the serpent; but where is the murderous
  fool?
[*Bang at portals.*]
Come!
[*Enter* ZABAK.]

ZABAK: Lord Nimri, O king!

KING DARIUS:
Now comes the murderous fool; the serpent said
  he'd come.

ZABAK: My king?

KING DARIUS [*turning to* HAJITHA]:
Did not the serpent say he would come?
Did not the serpent say, 'If I read the skies
As well as I play the harp, Nimri's greed
Will kill sleep and bring him here'?
[*He turns back to* ZABAK.]
What did the beast then do, Zabak?

Daniel

ZABAK: I understand not the king.

KING DARIUS:
It's a play, Zabak; a play. This is the serpent,
And this is the beast. And if you could only act,
You'd be the executioner, Zabak.
[*He turns to* HAJITHA.]
What do you think of my little plot –
Zabak as the play's executioner?
You are silent, my perfumed serpent, why?
[*He turns to* SATALA.]
And you, dearest adulterous beast,
What do you say of Zabak as executioner?
You tremble: I can hear the thumping of your heart
And the rattle-drumming of your bones and ribs.
Why? It is but a play, a little play.
[*He turns back to* ZABAK.]
Zabak, your scimitar!
[*He takes it.*]
And fetch yourself another from a guard;
If any manly limb or painted fingernail
Leaves this room without my nod to you, you die!

ZABAK: The king's word is done.

KING DARIUS:
Send in the next player: he waits in the wings;
His name is murderous fool, but he bears Nimri too.

ZABAK: As the king commands.
                    [*Exit.*
[KING DARIUS *inspects* SATALA *and* HAJITHA, ZABAK'S *scimitar menacing in his hand.*]

KING DARIUS: My players are silent, why?
[*Enter* NIMRI.]

NIMRI: Live for ever, O king!

KING DARIUS: Right on cue, murderous fool.

NIMRI: My king?

KING DARIUS:
It's a play of three conspiracies –
Here's the serpent and over there's the beast;

Daniel

You're the murderous fool, I'm the blind uxorious
   fool.
The serpent, the beast and the murderous fool
Conspire to relieve the king of Daniel,
Then the serpent and the beast conspire
To first relieve the king of his head,
And to then do the same to the murderous fool.
Then the serpent conspires with her heart
To relieve the beast of his head
And appoint herself monarch of Babylon,
Empress of the world! ...Your tongues are caught
   dead.
Why do you look at me so strangely? What smell is
   this?
Is it the smell of fear, or the smell of death?
Do you tremble? Why? This is but a play:
We do not die, we only play death.
Not even Daniel, not even Daniel dies...
[*Bang at portals,* ZABAK *appears immediately.*]

ZABAK: My king! My king! My king...
[*Enter* DANIEL.]

[*He stands at the door, silent. All eyes are transfixed on him. Utter silence for a while, then* ZABAK *continues...*]

Daniel ... Daniel is alive! He's alive, O king!

The lions ... the lions –

DANIEL:

The lions harmed me not; see, O king!

My God, the living God, whom I serve,

Sent His angel to seal the lions' mouths,

For I was found blameless in His sight,

And the beasts hurt me not, nor bruise nor scratch.

See, O king! See! I was found blameless before God;

And before you, O king, have I done wrong?

[*Pause.*]

[KING DARIUS *walks slowly to* DANIEL.]

KING DARIUS: Daniel ... Daniel...

[*He examines him, feeling his hand, his arm, etc.*]

It is indeed you...

[*Pause.*]

[*He embraces him, and then sinks to his knees before* DANIEL.]

Daniel, my chief minister, your God ... is ... God.
[*He rises and turns to the audience.*]
The God of Daniel is indeed God,
The living God enduring for ever!
His kingdom and dominion shall never end.
He delivers and rescues, works signs and wonders
In heaven and on earth, He who has saved Daniel
From the lions, and from death's unavailing power.
Praise be to this God! Praise be to Him!
Praise be to Him for ever and ever!
[*Pause.*]
Zabak!

ZABAK: Here I am, O king; ready to best ready!

KING DARIUS:

Daniel has come and now the play must end,
But first, play the falling sword of justice:
Take the serpent, the beast and the murderous fool,
And in just recompense, feed them to the lions,
For Daniel's God is a God of Justice,
And on that note must all come to an end.

[HAJITHA *lets out a cry and faints.*]

[NIMRI *rushes to his knife embedded in the table, but is balked by ZABAK who subdues him after a short struggle.*]

[SATALA *quietly draws out his knife.*]

SATALA [*coolly, with the knife poised over his breast*]:

Crude Nimri ever did lack stealth and style.

[*He stabs himself to death, despite ZABAK'S attempt to stop him.*]

KING DARIUS [*to* ZABAK]:

Alive or dead, to the lions with them!

[ZABAK *busies himself with the bodies.*]

[*Lights dim to near darkness.*]

[DANIEL *drops on one knee, hands raised to God in admiration. Spotlight on him for a moment.*]

Lights fail completely.

The End

About the Author

PHILIP BEGHO is the author of several award-winning books. His wide-ranging interest has seen him in a varied career that has spanned journalism, banking, business, legal practice and university teaching. He has also engaged in film and theatrical production.

He now works as a full-time writer, concentrating largely on children's literature and verse drama.

Daniel was 1st runner-up in the 1994 ANA drama competition, beaten only by the author's other verse play *Esther*.

Verse plays by Philip Begho

#1 Esther
#2 Daniel
#3 Job's Wife
#4 Jephthah's Daughter

www.ingramcontent.com/pod-product-compliance
Lightning Source LLC
Chambersburg PA
CBHW071216160426
43196CB00012B/2327